Max goes fishing

Story by Annette Smith
Illustrations by Richard Hoit

Max and Grandpa
sat down on the steps.

"I like going fishing
with you, Grandpa,"
said Max.

"This is a good day
for fishing," said Grandpa.
"We will get some big fish today.
Here is your fishing line, Max,
and here is my fishing line."

"Look Grandpa!" said Max.

"I can see some little fish."

Nibble, nibble, nibble
went the hungry little fish.

7

Max looked down at his line in the water.

"Where are the big fish, Grandpa?" said Max.
"They are not coming today."

The little fish came back
to Max's line.

Nibble, nibble, nibble
went the hungry little fish, again.

"Go away, little fish!"
said Max.

Grandpa looked at the shellfish on the step.

"A big fish will like this," he said.

Max and Grandpa
went on fishing.

"Grandpa! Grandpa!"
shouted Max.
"A fish is on my line."

15

"Look at my **big** fish!"
said Max.